THE

FIVE-A-DAY

SYSTEM

Created by an ADHD-er for people
who feel a lack of motivation but still
need to get sh*t done.

MANDY FROEHLICH

The Five-A-Day System
Mandy Froehlich

Copyright © 2024 by Mandy Froehlich.
Published by Mandy Froehlich
Educational Consulting, LLC
PO Box 150324, Alexandria, VA 22315
www.mandyfroehlich.com

For inquiries and details on bulk order pricing, contact the publisher: mandy@divergentedu.com

ISBN: 978-1-9593473-9-2

OVERVIEW OF THE SYSTEM

Why would you do this and what to
know before starting.

WHY THIS SYSTEM?

I've spent a lot of time trying to figure out how to motivate myself. Before this system, on the best days, I'd choose a few things I wanted to do and work on them, feeling somewhat successful for getting some work accomplished at the end of the day. Eventually, however, the things I didn't want to do would be put off until the last minute, and procrastination would send my stress level skyrocketing as I ignored all other duties in my life to get a project finished in the 11th hour. I'd tell people I work better under pressure, but what really happened is my Defcon Five stress level was so high that it drowned out the normal stress indicators that might slow me down. I needed a better system.

I tried other to-do lists and calendars both online and with cute little covers. They didn't work because I really did not know how to plan. Writing something down and developing an overwhelming list of tasks that needed to be done did nothing but stress me out more, and it wasn't helpful. I'd cherry-pick the things I actually wanted to do and eventually follow my ADHD down a rabbit hole for hours at a time. I was in "The Flow" all right. The Flow of having a brain full of useless information and still a whole list of tasks to accomplish to lead a productive life (and get paid). I needed something that wasn't going to take me extra time, that would help me to feel successful more often, and that would help me fight against my tendency to procrastinate because I was so freaking over being stressed.

Over time, I was able to develop the Five-A-Day system. To look at the weekly pages you may think that it is a simple plan where you just write down five tasks a day that must be completed. That's not exactly true. There are rules. To keep the system sustainable, there needs to be a mix of tasks that will be able to be accomplished daily.

I challenge you to try the system as-is for a month. Then, make changes that fit you. Get that dopamine, the happy "reward" chemical in your brain, flowing every time you check something off. Over time, it will get easier and easier to finish five a day!

HOW ARE YOU FEELING?

You may be feeling a mixture of excitement and "I hope this works" because how many other times have you tried strategies to get motivated? If you're like me, the hopeful optimism can be short-lived when you're overwhelmed. Here are some daily intentions related to motivation that might help.

- Today, I choose to focus on what truly matters and let go of the rest. I will prioritize tasks that align with my goals and bring me joy, knowing that progress, not perfection, is the key.
- I acknowledge my strength and resilience. Today, I commit to taking small, manageable steps toward my goals, trusting that each step forward is a victory in its own right.
- Today, I embrace flexibility and grace. I understand that not everything may go as planned, but I am capable of adapting and finding solutions. My journey is unique, and so is my path to productivity.
- I give myself permission to be proud of my progress today, no matter how big or small. Each task I complete is a testament to my commitment and effort, and I celebrate my dedication to growth.
- Today, I choose to approach my tasks with a positive mindset, knowing that my attitude can transform challenges into opportunities for learning and growth. I am in control of how I respond to my day.

BENEFITS OF THE SYSTEM

Brain Space
By writing down your to-do list and keeping a running list, you're clearing garbage out of your head and providing yourself with extra brain space.

An Ongoing Task List
No more wasting time by sitting down and deciding what you need to do, getting overwhelmed by everything, and then not doing anything. Instead, all your tasks are already written down and planned day-to-day. All you need to do is finish them.

A Reduction in Procrastination
By breaking up projects into smaller pieces and working them into daily tasks, projects can be completed without procrastination and with less stress.

Ability to Give Timelines
Before using this system, I had an issue when people would ask me when a task could be done. Being an ultimate people-pleaser with no sense of time, I would tell them "Tomorrow." Then that task would need to be done before everything else because I had given them that day, even though I really didn't have time to do it. With the Five-A-Day system, I had an ongoing list and could tell someone quickly when a task could actually be done by looking at my planner and finding the next available spot. It could be one of the last-minute openings that I left that week or it could be added to the back of the list depending on its importance. Either way, it becomes easier to estimate when a task will be completed without overloading yourself.

TIPS & ADVICE

You may still have some reservations or questions about the system. Below, I've preemptively anticipated what concerns you might have.

"I'm trying this because I feel super overwhelmed by life."

I totally get it. When I first developed the system, I started with three-a-day. I wanted to be sure that I could get something done in a day, yet five felt overwhelming. That might be another place to start. Another option would be to use five a day but alternate the number of Tier One and Tier Two that are in a day. For example, maybe you start with 4 - Tier One and 1 - Tier Two and work your way up to having more Tier Twos. In these cases, I always think it's better to have something than to get to the end of the day and have nothing.

"Just tell me what I need to do."

You need to create your five-a-day and stick to it. No system can force you to finish the five tasks you've written down in a day. However, if you commit to finishing those five tasks (and have a plan in place if you don't) you'll need to think less about things that need to get done and more about activities you like to do.

"I don't like all the rules. "

Yeah, I get that. I don't like being put in a box either. However, you have more choices in the system than you do rules. You can choose how to break up your Tier Three projects. You can choose how many of each Tier you put on a day. You can choose to use appointments as tasks. You can even choose to work ahead or choose when you stop working (understanding that anything you don't get accomplished will need to be done on the weekend). You can choose to add fewer tasks to a day if you're having trouble even accomplishing five things because you're struggling. The rules help you stay on track.

"I have more to do than just five things."

The system is created for people who are struggling to get stuff done and feel motivated. It's meant to increase the feelings of success in a day until they feel like they can do it on their own (although I find myself coming back to the system often because it works for me). Other things might also be accomplished in a day - checking emails, replying to emails quickly that aren't on the task list, scheduling a personal appointment that wasn't on the list...but these five things need to be done to move forward in your world. Should you leave work if you're scheduled until 5 pm and you're done with your list? I wouldn't recommend it. However, if you finish your list you can feel confident that you're making progress, and that's the point. Also, you can always choose to work ahead on a future day's list.

"Ok. But five just doesn't seem like very much."

I know it doesn't sound like much, but how often do you cross 25 tasks a week off your to do list? How often are you leaving big chunks of a project until the last minute? What you check off starts to add up, and you'll feel more successful when you look back at what you accomplished over the week. And the first time you finish a project well before the due date, I want to see a celebration shout-out on social media so I can celebrate with you!

GETTING STARTED

You get to write your tasks down.
Unlimited checkboxes await.

CREATE YOUR TASK LIST

The first step in the system is to create an initial task list. This list is going to help you fill out your Five-A-Day planner pages.

To get started, you first need to write down everything you can think of that you need to do. If you work, your tasks may be a mix of professional and personal. You should write down everything you can think of - important emails or phone calls that may take time, projects, running to the store to buy a birthday present...the tasks that have been floating around in your brain taking up space.

To facilitate this process there is a workbook-style page provided after you've read the directions as well as a digital version if you prefer to work through it online. This part may take a bit of time but I promise there will be so many boxes to check off! You're going to love it!

I often get asked the question, "What type of tasks should be written down?" For example, I was working through the system with a client and he asked about writing down the task of "grocery shopping" which was something he did weekly. What you consider a written task is a very gray area, but there are a few guidelines that you might find helpful.

TASK TIPS

In general, tasks that are just a part of being a human are not written down. Tasks like "taking a shower," "doing the dishes," or "putting the kids to bed" would not be tasks that are added to the list. Remember, we do so much more in a day than five tasks so ideally what you put on the list should move you forward instead of keeping you stagnant.

The exception to this guideline is when you have a special reason to do a normal task. An example would be something like this: you are inviting people to your house for a birthday party. Then, tasks like "clean the house" and "decorate for the party" would appear on the task list because they're special instances of a normal task.

TASK TIPS

Tasks that are repeated can also be put onto the list. For example, one day out of the month is a *Bill and Business* day for me. It's where I handle all the business tasks for the house and business.

Tasks on that list might be "Pay bills," "Sort mail," or "Balance accounts." Even though I complete them every month, they still take enough time to be put on the list. Another example is that I am responsible for two newsletters that go out at various times of the month. These tasks also go onto my Five-A-Day.

Ultimately, what you write down for your tasks is up to you. I will also add this if you are really struggling: if you are doom-scrolling social media and spending copious amounts of time on the couch and you're starting the Five-A-Day from a place that feels like even five tasks in total for a day is overwhelming, then my suggestion is to do what you need to do just to get started. If that means writing down tasks that wouldn't normally be written down or only starting with three tasks, that's okay. Stressing yourself out isn't going to help. Give yourself grace, time, and an easy start. Don't forget to celebrate what you accomplished instead of feeling guilty over what you didn't.

Next, we are going to label the tasks on our list. Unlike some lists where they might have you label them as work or personal, fun or not fun, etc., we are going to label them by tiers. The tiers are as follows:

Tier One

Tasks that may take between 15 minutes and 30 minutes.

Tier Two

Tasks that will take longer - like an hour to an hour and a half or two hours.

Tier Three

Projects or tasks that will take longer than two hours to complete.

Look at the list you made and begin to mark each task as Tier One, Two, or Three. If you find something that doesn't seem to fit, just decide and put it somewhere for now. As you understand the system better, you may go back and change it later. That's okay.

Also, mark if it is a repeated task and if the task has a due date. You'll use this information when you transfer the task to the Five-A-Day planner pages.

Use the following workbook page to help create your initial task list. You can also go to https://bit.ly/initialtasklist or use the QR code to access a digital version of this resource. You will need a Google account to do so.

A COMMON PITFALL

When you begin planning for tasks, it's common to miscalculate how long tasks will take, especially when you move into Tier Three tasks. This can throw off your entire week especially if the task has a looming due date. For example, I recently had to create a website page for a project that I felt would be a Tier Two task. I figured it would be approximately 1.5 hours. It took me eight hours and was due by the end of the week. What should have been one Tier Two Monday task essentially took me more than a whole day of tasks.

Here were some of the problems from the start:
- What needed to be accomplished on the page I had never done before, therefore, I had no idea how long it was going to take.
- I had to research some parts of the task I wasn't expecting.
- I hadn't broken the website project up into small enough tasks.

After using the system for a while, this part will become more natural. However, when you're thinking about task time, especially when you're dealing with Tier Three, give yourself a cushion. The worst that happens is you finish the project early.

Here are some guidelines to help you out.
- If you haven't done the task or project before, consider adding research time to learn how to do it first.
- Add the research task early to the planner so if you find you need more time you have the room to extend it.
- Plan double the amount of time to finish it, especially if you've never done it before.

Until you've been using the system for a while new tasks may need some additional thought and planning.

INITIAL TASK LIST

Task Description	Tier	Ongoing or Repeated?	Due Date
☐	1 2 3		
☐	1 2 3		
☐	1 2 3		
☐	1 2 3		
☐	1 2 3		
☐	1 2 3		
☐	1 2 3		
☐	1 2 3		
☐	1 2 3		
☐	1 2 3		
☐	1 2 3		
☐	1 2 3		
☐	1 2 3		
☐	1 2 3		
☐	1 2 3		
☐	1 2 3		
☐	1 2 3		
☐	1 2 3		
☐	1 2 3		
☐	1 2 3		

INITIAL TASK LIST

Task Description	Tier	Ongoing or Repeated?	Due Date
☐	1 2 3		
☐	1 2 3		
☐	1 2 3		
☐	1 2 3		
☐	1 2 3		
☐	1 2 3		
☐	1 2 3		
☐	1 2 3		
☐	1 2 3		
☐	1 2 3		
☐	1 2 3		
☐	1 2 3		
☐	1 2 3		
☐	1 2 3		
☐	1 2 3		
☐	1 2 3		
☐	1 2 3		
☐	1 2 3		
☐	1 2 3		

ORGANIZE TIER THREE

If you're like me, Tier Three are the tasks I would typically procrastinate on. This may be for a few reasons: maybe I don't know where or how to get started, maybe I find it boring, maybe I finished some of it but the rest seems redundant and I get sick of looking at it. Whatever the reason, they need to be broken down into smaller, manageable tasks.

So, the next step is to take the Tier Three tasks and projects that you've identified in the Initial Task List and break them down into Tier One and Tier Two tasks. For example, a project might be broken down like this:

Project: Prepare for Webinar

Tier One	Tier Two
→ Email webinar host for questions	→ Plan question answers
→ Read through questions	→ Create content for presentation
→ Write outline for presentation	→ Add images and videos to slides
→ Presentation run-through #1	
→ Run-through #2	

Once the project has been broken down into Tier One and Tier Two, you'll better be able to add them to the planner to avoid procrastinating and spending all day on one project.

TIER THREE BREAKDOWN

Project	Task Description	Tier	Due Date
☐		1 2	
☐		1 2	
☐		1 2	
☐		1 2	
☐		1 2	
☐		1 2	
☐		1 2	
☐		1 2	
☐		1 2	
☐		1 2	
☐		1 2	
☐		1 2	
☐		1 2	
☐		1 2	
☐		1 2	
☐		1 2	
☐		1 2	
☐		1 2	
☐		1 2	
☐		1 2	

ADD TASKS TO PLANNER

Begin adding the tasks to your planner by first noting any meetings or appointments you have in the "Schedule" space if you know them. It can be as general or specific as you would like. I keep my entire schedule in Google Calendar, so my appointment notation might look like this:

Five-a-Day Weekly Planner

Week:

Schedule

12 M		Webinar
☐ Appointments		Doctor
☐		appointment
☐		Meeting
☐		
☐		

This is important because rule #1 for the system is:

For every three meetings or appointments in a day, you can choose to use them as a task. If there are two or fewer, they don't get added as a task unless they are meetings over an hour long. Last-minute meetings or appointments are the only time that tasks should be moved around on the planner.

This is simply because of time. If you are attending meetings, you cannot also be working on tasks. In groups of three, these appointments or meetings are considered a Tier Two task.

Then, start adding your Tier One and Tier Two tasks by following Rule #2 of the system:

Add tasks in following a 2/3 or 3/2 format. Each day should have either:
2 - Tier One and 3 - Tier Two tasks (known as 2/3 format)
OR
3 - Tier One and 2 - Tier Two Tasks (known as 3/2 format)

Again, this is simply because of time. Don't forget to add in the tasks from the projects that need to be done. Try to avoid putting too many of the tasks of a project on one day so you don't burn yourself out on that project. You can choose to use 2/3 or 3/2 daily. You do not always need to follow one of the formats and can switch back and forth depending on the day.

 When deciding on the priority for your tasks follow this order:
1. Repeated tasks
2. Tasks with due dates
3. Remaining tasks

Continue filling out Monday through Friday while observing Rule #3:

Leave two open task spaces per week for last minute task additions or changes in schedule that involves moving tasks to accommodate meetings.

As you add tasks from your Initial Task List to your Five-A-Day planner pages, use the checkboxes provided on the workbook pages to keep track of the tasks you've moved over.

INITIAL TASK LIST

Task Description	Tier	Ongoing or Repeated?	Due Date
☐ Email boss documents from project	① 2 3	N	
☐ Develop content for presentation	1 ② 3	N	
☐ Create high-level outline for new course	① 2 3	N	12/15
☐ Create marketing plan for presentation	1 ② 3	N	1/10
☐ Monthly newsletter	1 ② 3	Y	First of every month

Five-a-Day Weekly Planner

Week:

Schedule

	12 M	
Tier Two	☐ Appointments	Grocery shopping
Tier One	☐ Email boss documents from project	
Tier Two	☐ Develop content for presentation	Doctor appointment
Tier One	☐ Create high level outline for new course	
Tier Two	☐ Create marketing plan for presentation	Meeting

WEEKENDS

Let's say that you have struggled to get stuff done during the week. Well, then you will need to follow Rules #4:

What you don't finish during the week needs to be finished on the weekend.

Is it a punishment? Well, I prefer to call it a consequence. If this rule wasn't in place, you could continue moving tasks all around and the system wouldn't work. Really, it's only five things a day that have been broken down into smaller things AND you had two days with only four tasks to accommodate for other tasks. Barring a complete emergency or a massive sickness, expecting to finish the list on the weekend is reasonable.

On the flip side, if you finish everything on your list, you have accomplished at least 25 tasks during the week that needed to be done! That is amazing! In that case, you deserve the weekend off. Do something fun that wouldn't go on a task list.

Which brings us to our final rule #5:

Do not cherry-pick from the week. You must finish the tasks on the day you wrote them (but you can complete them in any order).

PROJECTS & REMEMBER ME

The project section is to list projects that are ongoing. It's to be used to remember the projects that are being included on the task list. As they are finished, they can be removed from the projects section.

Remember me is for those little things you need to remember throughout the week. Maybe it's a phone number or a project that isn't included in tasks yet but needs to be added. There are also pages added after each week for notes or thoughts.

NEXT STEPS

When you're done with setup, you'll start to carry the planner with you so you can continue to add tasks as they come up. First, you'll quickly determine if the task is a Tier One or Tier Two, and then you'll add it to the next day in the planner that makes sense. If it's a Tier Three project, then you'll take the time to break it down and add it to the planner as smaller tasks. Remember, the five things you've accomplished in a day might not be the only things you do, but they are the things that need to be done.

Use the system and planner faithfully for one month. Then, do a one-month audit on your implementation. You may find you need to make changes. That's okay. Make the tweaks. Use these questions to help guide your thinking:

- Am I correctly estimating how long it takes me to complete tasks?
- How does the system need to adjust to work for me?
- Are there tasks that I originally added that I'm finding I don't need on my planner anymore? Was there something that I was missing?

Your initial setup may go out for WEEKS. Do NOT freak out. These tasks were all the things you had on your to-do list or floating in your head that were not getting done before and now you have a plan. You're starting with the tasks that have due dates, you have room in your weeks for last-minute additions, and the rest of the tasks now have a home. It may feel scary but it's actually amazing.

REVIEW OF THE RULES

Rule #1: For every three meetings or appointments in a day, you can choose to use them as a task. If there are fewer than two, they don't get added as a task. Meetings or appointments are the only time that tasks should be moved around on the planner.

Rule #2: Add tasks in following a 2/3 format. Each day should have either 2 - Tier One and 3 - Tier Two tasks **OR** 3 - Tier One and 2 - Tier Two Tasks.

Rule #3: Leave two open task spaces per week for last-minute task additions or changes in schedule that involve moving tasks to accommodate meetings.

Rule #4: What you don't finish during the week needs to be finished on the weekend.

Rule #5: Do not cherry-pick from the week. You must finish the tasks each day on the day you wrote them (but you can complete them in any order).

SEE AN EXAMPLE

Then get started.

(Also, look at all those opportunities for check marks!)

Five-a-Day Weekly Planner

Schedule

---

12 M	
☑ Appointments	Grocery shopping
☑ Email boss documents from project	
☑ Develop content for presentation	Doctor appointment
☑ Create high level outline for new course	
☑ Create marketing plan for presentation	Meeting

13 T	
☐ Create proposal for Adobe	Meeting
☐ Fill out new W-9 for business	Meeting
☐ Spend one hour searching small business grants	
☐ Create graphics for marketing plan	
☐ Create copy for marketing plan	

14 W	
☐ Email proposal to Adobe	
☐ Email marketing plan w/ description to social media person	
☐ Spend one hour on research for course	
☐ Add images to presentation	
☐ [Open task for last minute additions]	

15 TH

- [ ] Appointments
- [ ] Add detailed outline to high level course outline
- [ ] Do first run through of presentation
- [ ] Sign up for platform for course
- [ ] [Open task for last minute additions]

Dentist

Meeting

Meeting

16 F

- [ ] Email resources to colleague
- [ ] Review conference descriptions for colleague
- [ ] Do second run through of presentation
- [ ] Add research to course outline
- [ ] Create graphic for course

17 Saturday

Pickleball

18 Sunday

Current Projects

Presentation

New course

Adobe project

Remember Me:

Add new Fundraising project tasks to planner

Five-a-Day Weekly Planner

Schedule

4/29 M
- [x] Submit a book review for Mandy
- [ ] Finish Google course + study ~1 hour
- [ ] Work on STEAM makers 2nd Edition proposal
- [ ] Good will drop off
- [ ] work on Edutopia revisions

4/30 T
- [x] Travel Day
- [ ] Study for Google Test
- [ ] Edutopia revisions
- [x] Ready for tomorrow
- [x] RVG meeting

5/1 W
- [ ] Work Day
- [ ]
- [ ]
- [ ]
- [ ] Study for Google

5/2 TH

- [ ] Work Day
- [ ]
- [ ]
- [ ]
- [ ] Drive to Little Rock

5/3 F

- [ ] Fly Home
- [ ]
- [ ]
- [ ] Submit Edutopia
- [ ] Study for Google

Saturday

Mother's Day plans
Nicole B-day plan

Sunday

Current Projects

Remember Me:
Schedule w/ Phoebe
Reschedule Lauren

NOTES

NOTES

Five-a-Day Weekly Planner

Week:

Schedule

5/6 **M**
☐ Travel Day
☐
☐
☐
☐

5/7 **T**
☐ Work Day
☐
☐ ↓
☐
☐

5/8 **W**
☐ Work Day
☐
☐ ↓
☐
☐

5/9 TH

- [ ] Google cert study
- [ ]
- [ ]
- [ ]
- [ ]

5/10 F

- [ ] clean house
- [ ] Good will Drop off
- [ ]
- [ ]
- [ ] Color Run?

Saturday

Sunday

Current Projects

Remember Me:

NOTES

NOTES

Five-a-Day Weekly Planner

Week:

Schedule

M
- [ ]
- [ ]
- [ ]
- [ ]
- [ ]

T
- [ ]
- [ ]
- [ ]
- [ ]
- [ ]

W
- [ ]
- [ ]
- [ ]
- [ ]
- [ ]

TH

- [ ]
- [ ]
- [ ]
- [ ]
- [ ]

F

- [ ]
- [ ]
- [ ]
- [ ]
- [ ]

Saturday

Sunday

Current Projects

Remember Me:

NOTES

NOTES

Five-a-Day Weekly Planner

Week:

Schedule

M

- [ ]
- [ ]
- [ ]
- [ ]
- [ ]

T

- [ ]
- [ ]
- [ ]
- [ ]
- [ ]

W

- [ ]
- [ ]
- [ ]
- [ ]
- [ ]

TH

- [ ]
- [ ]
- [ ]
- [ ]
- [ ]

F

- [ ]
- [ ]
- [ ]
- [ ]
- [ ]

Saturday

Sunday

Current Projects

Remember Me:

NOTES

NOTES

Five-a-Day Weekly Planner

Schedule

M

- [ ]
- [ ]
- [ ]
- [ ]
- [ ]

T

- [ ]
- [ ]
- [ ]
- [ ]
- [ ]

W

- [ ]
- [ ]
- [ ]
- [ ]
- [ ]

TH

- [ ]
- [ ]
- [ ]
- [ ]
- [ ]

F

- [ ]
- [ ]
- [ ]
- [ ]
- [ ]

Saturday

Sunday

Current Projects

Remember Me:

NOTES

NOTES

Five-a-Day Weekly Planner

Week:

Schedule

M

- [ ]
- [ ]
- [ ]
- [ ]
- [ ]

T

- [ ]
- [ ]
- [ ]
- [ ]
- [ ]

W

- [ ]
- [ ]
- [ ]
- [ ]
- [ ]

TH

- [ ]
- [ ]
- [ ]
- [ ]
- [ ]

F

- [ ]
- [ ]
- [ ]
- [ ]
- [ ]

Saturday

Sunday

Current Projects

Remember Me:

NOTES

NOTES

Five-a-Day Weekly Planner

Week:

Schedule

M

- [ ]
- [ ]
- [ ]
- [ ]
- [ ]

T

- [ ]
- [ ]
- [ ]
- [ ]
- [ ]

W

- [ ]
- [ ]
- [ ]
- [ ]
- [ ]

TH

- [ ]
- [ ]
- [ ]
- [ ]
- [ ]

F

- [ ]
- [ ]
- [ ]
- [ ]
- [ ]

Saturday

Sunday

Current Projects

Remember Me:

NOTES

NOTES

Five-a-Day Weekly Planner

Week:

Schedule

M

- [ ]
- [ ]
- [ ]
- [ ]
- [ ]

T

- [ ]
- [ ]
- [ ]
- [ ]
- [ ]

W

- [ ]
- [ ]
- [ ]
- [ ]
- [ ]

TH

- [ ]
- [ ]
- [ ]
- [ ]
- [ ]

F

- [ ]
- [ ]
- [ ]
- [ ]
- [ ]

Saturday

Sunday

Current Projects

Remember Me:

NOTES

NOTES

Five-a-Day Weekly Planner

Week:

Schedule

M

- [ ]
- [ ]
- [ ]
- [ ]
- [ ]

T

- [ ]
- [ ]
- [ ]
- [ ]
- [ ]

W

- [ ]
- [ ]
- [ ]
- [ ]
- [ ]

TH

- [ ]
- [ ]
- [ ]
- [ ]
- [ ]

F

- [ ]
- [ ]
- [ ]
- [ ]
- [ ]

Saturday

Sunday

Current Projects

Remember Me:

NOTES

NOTES

Five-a-Day Weekly Planner

Week:

Schedule

M

- [ ]
- [ ]
- [ ]
- [ ]
- [ ]

T

- [ ]
- [ ]
- [ ]
- [ ]
- [ ]

W

- [ ]
- [ ]
- [ ]
- [ ]
- [ ]

TH

- [ ]
- [ ]
- [ ]
- [ ]
- [ ]

F

- [ ]
- [ ]
- [ ]
- [ ]
- [ ]

Saturday

Sunday

Current Projects

Remember Me:

NOTES

NOTES

Five-a-Day Weekly Planner

Week:

Schedule

M

- [ ]
- [ ]
- [ ]
- [ ]
- [ ]

T

- [ ]
- [ ]
- [ ]
- [ ]
- [ ]

W

- [ ]
- [ ]
- [ ]
- [ ]
- [ ]

TH

- [ ]
- [ ]
- [ ]
- [ ]
- [ ]

F

- [ ]
- [ ]
- [ ]
- [ ]
- [ ]

Saturday

Sunday

Current Projects

Remember Me:

NOTES

NOTES

Five-a-Day Weekly Planner

Week:

Schedule

M

- [ ]
- [ ]
- [ ]
- [ ]
- [ ]

T

- [ ]
- [ ]
- [ ]
- [ ]
- [ ]

W

- [ ]
- [ ]
- [ ]
- [ ]
- [ ]

TH

- [ ]
- [ ]
- [ ]
- [ ]
- [ ]

F

- [ ]
- [ ]
- [ ]
- [ ]
- [ ]

Saturday

Sunday

Current Projects

Remember Me:

NOTES

NOTES

Five-a-Day Weekly Planner

Week:

Schedule

M

- [ ]
- [ ]
- [ ]
- [ ]
- [ ]

T

- [ ]
- [ ]
- [ ]
- [ ]
- [ ]

W

- [ ]
- [ ]
- [ ]
- [ ]
- [ ]

TH

- [ ]
- [ ]
- [ ]
- [ ]
- [ ]

F

- [ ]
- [ ]
- [ ]
- [ ]
- [ ]

Saturday

Sunday

Current Projects

Remember Me:

NOTES

NOTES

Five-a-Day Weekly Planner

Week:

Schedule

M

- [ ]
- [ ]
- [ ]
- [ ]
- [ ]

T

- [ ]
- [ ]
- [ ]
- [ ]
- [ ]

W

- [ ]
- [ ]
- [ ]
- [ ]
- [ ]

TH

- [ ]
- [ ]
- [ ]
- [ ]
- [ ]

F

- [ ]
- [ ]
- [ ]
- [ ]
- [ ]

Saturday

Sunday

Current Projects

Remember Me:

NOTES

NOTES

Five-a-Day Weekly Planner

Week:

Schedule

M

- [ ]
- [ ]
- [ ]
- [ ]
- [ ]

T

- [ ]
- [ ]
- [ ]
- [ ]
- [ ]

W

- [ ]
- [ ]
- [ ]
- [ ]
- [ ]

TH

- [ ]
- [ ]
- [ ]
- [ ]
- [ ]

F

- [ ]
- [ ]
- [ ]
- [ ]
- [ ]

Saturday

Sunday

Current Projects

Remember Me:

NOTES

NOTES

Five-a-Day Weekly Planner

Week:

Schedule

M
- [ ]
- [ ]
- [ ]
- [ ]
- [ ]

T
- [ ]
- [ ]
- [ ]
- [ ]
- [ ]

W
- [ ]
- [ ]
- [ ]
- [ ]
- [ ]

TH

- [ ]
- [ ]
- [ ]
- [ ]
- [ ]

F

- [ ]
- [ ]
- [ ]
- [ ]
- [ ]

Saturday

Sunday

Current Projects

Remember Me:

NOTES

NOTES

Five-a-Day Weekly Planner

Week:

Schedule

M

- [ ]
- [ ]
- [ ]
- [ ]
- [ ]

T

- [ ]
- [ ]
- [ ]
- [ ]
- [ ]

W

- [ ]
- [ ]
- [ ]
- [ ]
- [ ]

TH

- [ ]
- [ ]
- [ ]
- [ ]
- [ ]

F

- [ ]
- [ ]
- [ ]
- [ ]
- [ ]

Saturday

Sunday

Current Projects

Remember Me:

NOTES

NOTES

Five-a-Day Weekly Planner

Week:

Schedule

M

- [ ]
- [ ]
- [ ]
- [ ]
- [ ]

T

- [ ]
- [ ]
- [ ]
- [ ]
- [ ]

W

- [ ]
- [ ]
- [ ]
- [ ]
- [ ]

TH

- [ ]
- [ ]
- [ ]
- [ ]
- [ ]

F

- [ ]
- [ ]
- [ ]
- [ ]
- [ ]

Saturday

Sunday

Current Projects

Remember Me:

NOTES

NOTES

Five-a-Day Weekly Planner

Week:

Schedule

M

- [ ]
- [ ]
- [ ]
- [ ]
- [ ]

T

- [ ]
- [ ]
- [ ]
- [ ]
- [ ]

W

- [ ]
- [ ]
- [ ]
- [ ]
- [ ]

TH

- [ ]
- [ ]
- [ ]
- [ ]
- [ ]

F

- [ ]
- [ ]
- [ ]
- [ ]
- [ ]

Saturday

Sunday

Current Projects

Remember Me:

NOTES

NOTES

Five-a-Day Weekly Planner

Week:

Schedule

M

- [ ]
- [ ]
- [ ]
- [ ]
- [ ]

T

- [ ]
- [ ]
- [ ]
- [ ]
- [ ]

W

- [ ]
- [ ]
- [ ]
- [ ]
- [ ]

TH

- [ ]
- [ ]
- [ ]
- [ ]
- [ ]

F

- [ ]
- [ ]
- [ ]
- [ ]
- [ ]

Saturday

Sunday

Current Projects

Remember Me:

NOTES

NOTES

Five-a-Day Weekly Planner

Week:

Schedule

M
- [ ]
- [ ]
- [ ]
- [ ]
- [ ]

T
- [ ]
- [ ]
- [ ]
- [ ]
- [ ]

W
- [ ]
- [ ]
- [ ]
- [ ]
- [ ]

TH

- [ ]
- [ ]
- [ ]
- [ ]
- [ ]

F

- [ ]
- [ ]
- [ ]
- [ ]
- [ ]

Saturday

Sunday

Current Projects

Remember Me:

NOTES

NOTES

Five-a-Day Weekly Planner

Week:

Schedule

M
- [ ]
- [ ]
- [ ]
- [ ]
- [ ]

T
- [ ]
- [ ]
- [ ]
- [ ]
- [ ]

W
- [ ]
- [ ]
- [ ]
- [ ]
- [ ]

TH

- [ ]
- [ ]
- [ ]
- [ ]
- [ ]

F

- [ ]
- [ ]
- [ ]
- [ ]
- [ ]

Saturday

Sunday

Current Projects

Remember Me:

NOTES

NOTES

Five-a-Day Weekly Planner

Week:

Schedule

M
- [ ]
- [ ]
- [ ]
- [ ]
- [ ]

T
- [ ]
- [ ]
- [ ]
- [ ]
- [ ]

W
- [ ]
- [ ]
- [ ]
- [ ]
- [ ]

TH

- [ ]
- [ ]
- [ ]
- [ ]
- [ ]

F

- [ ]
- [ ]
- [ ]
- [ ]
- [ ]

Saturday

Sunday

Current Projects

Remember Me:

NOTES

NOTES

Five-a-Day Weekly Planner

Week:

M

- [ ]
- [ ]
- [ ]
- [ ]
- [ ]

T

- [ ]
- [ ]
- [ ]
- [ ]
- [ ]

W

- [ ]
- [ ]
- [ ]
- [ ]
- [ ]

TH

- [ ]
- [ ]
- [ ]
- [ ]
- [ ]

F

- [ ]
- [ ]
- [ ]
- [ ]
- [ ]

Saturday

Sunday

Current Projects

Remember Me:

NOTES

NOTES

Five-a-Day Weekly Planner

Week:

Schedule

M
- [ ]
- [ ]
- [ ]
- [ ]
- [ ]

T
- [ ]
- [ ]
- [ ]
- [ ]
- [ ]

W
- [ ]
- [ ]
- [ ]
- [ ]
- [ ]

TH

- [ ]
- [ ]
- [ ]
- [ ]
- [ ]

F

- [ ]
- [ ]
- [ ]
- [ ]
- [ ]

Saturday

Sunday

Current Projects

Remember Me:

NOTES

NOTES

Five-a-Day Weekly Planner

Week:

Schedule

M
- [ ]
- [ ]
- [ ]
- [ ]
- [ ]

T
- [ ]
- [ ]
- [ ]
- [ ]
- [ ]

W
- [ ]
- [ ]
- [ ]
- [ ]
- [ ]

TH

- [ ]
- [ ]
- [ ]
- [ ]
- [ ]

F

- [ ]
- [ ]
- [ ]
- [ ]
- [ ]

Saturday

Sunday

Current Projects

Remember Me:

NOTES

NOTES

SIX MONTH
MARK

You just finished six months of the
Five-A-Day system.

That's **650 tasks** that you've
crossed off your list.

That's **650 good feelings** because
you've accomplished something.

Congratulations! Keep going!

If you'd like to order another book without the Five-A-Day
system directions and more weeks of planner, please
contact me at mandy@divergentedu.com.

ABOUT THE AUTHOR

Mandy Froehlich is an educator, consultant, author, and mental health advocate known predominantly for her work in education. She developed the Five-A-Day system as a coping mechanism as a result of undiagnosed ADHD.

Once the system was formed and the diagnosis was made, Froehlich shares her insights into getting sh*t done *in spite of* a propensity for procrastination and doom scrolling. Find out more about Froehlich on her website www.mandyfroehlich.com.

Please consider supporting this book by sharing it with others. If you have questions, concerns, or a compliment please email mandy@divergentedu.com.

Printed in the USA
CPSIA information can be obtained
at www.ICGtesting.com
CBHW041225140424
6901CB00026B/1861